Girls' Health™

Yeast Infections, Trichomoniasis, and Toxic Shock Syndrome

Michael Sommers

rosen publishing's
rosen central®

New York

Published in 2008 by The Rosen Publishing Group, Inc.
29 East 21st Street, New York, NY 10010

Library of Congress Cataloging-in-Publication Data

Sommers, Michael A., 1966–
Yeast infections, trichomoniasis, and toxic shock syndrome / Michael Sommers.—
1st ed.
     p. cm.—(Girls' health)
Includes bibliographical references and index.
ISBN-13: 978-1-4042-1951-9
ISBN-10: 1-4042-1951-X
1. Vagina—Infections—Juvenile literature. 2. Candidiasis, Vulvovaginal—Juvenile literature. 3. Trichomoniasis—Juvenile literature. 4. Toxic shock syndrome—Juvenile literature.
I. Title.
RG268.S66 2008
618.1'5—dc22

                                                                                    2007005609

Manufactured in the United States of America

Cover, pp. 1, 3, 4, 5, 22 © www.istockphoto.com; p. 7 © Educational Images/ Custom Medical Stock Photo; pp. 9, 33 CDC; p. 12 © Custom Medical Stock Photo; p. 13 © SIU BioMed/Custom Medical Stock Photo; p. 16 © www.istockphoto.com/ Andrei Tchernov; p. 18 © Paul J. Richards/AFP/Getty Images; p. 20 © Leonard Lessin/Photo Researchers, Inc.; p. 26 © Caroline von Tuempling/Iconica/Getty Images; p. 27 © www.istockphoto.com/annedde; p. 29 © www.istockphoto.com/Michael Bennett; p. 31 © Leonard Lessin/Peter Arnold, Inc.; p. 32 © www.istockphoto.com/ Soubrette; p. 35 © www.istockphoto.com/Ingvald Kaldhussaeter; p. 38 James Gathany/ CDC; p. 40 © Michael Newman/PhotoEdit, Inc.

Designer: Evelyn Horovicz; **Editor:** Kathy Campbell;
Photo Researcher: Amy Feinberg

Contents

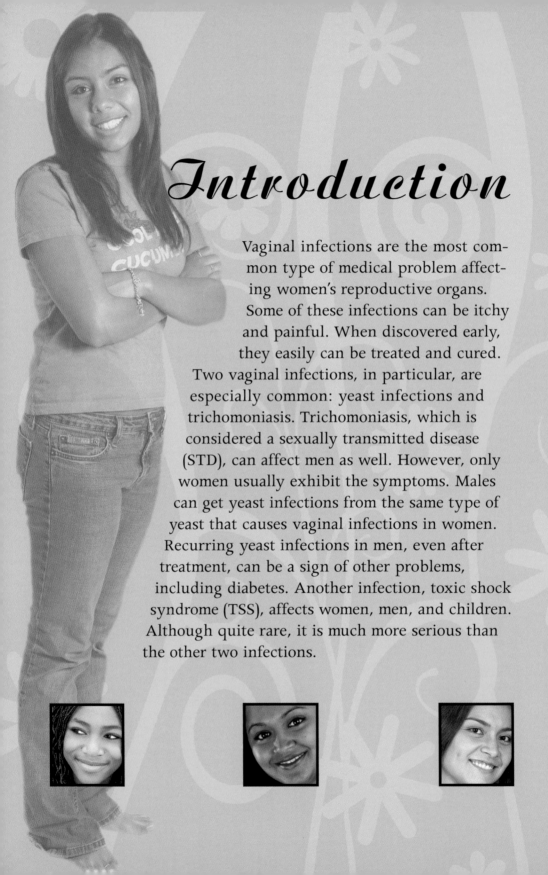

Introduction

Vaginal infections are the most common type of medical problem affecting women's reproductive organs. Some of these infections can be itchy and painful. When discovered early, they easily can be treated and cured. Two vaginal infections, in particular, are especially common: yeast infections and trichomoniasis. Trichomoniasis, which is considered a sexually transmitted disease (STD), can affect men as well. However, only women usually exhibit the symptoms. Males can get yeast infections from the same type of yeast that causes vaginal infections in women. Recurring yeast infections in men, even after treatment, can be a sign of other problems, including diabetes. Another infection, toxic shock syndrome (TSS), affects women, men, and children. Although quite rare, it is much more serious than the other two infections.

Both men and women often confuse the symptoms for yeast infections with some STDs and other infections. Consequently, it is best to visit your doctor for a diagnosis if you suspect that you have an infection. Any health problem should be treated by a physician and never neglected.

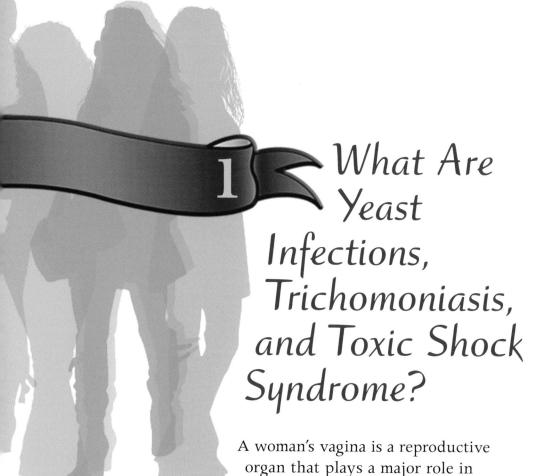

What Are Yeast Infections, Trichomoniasis, and Toxic Shock Syndrome?

A woman's vagina is a reproductive organ that plays a major role in menstruation, sexual intercourse, and childbirth. It is also a complex and sensitive part of the body. As you probably know, the vagina is the opening that is located between the urethra (urine canal) and the anus. The opening is called an orifice, as are other openings in your body such as your mouth and nostrils. Women tend to be less familiar with their sexual organs than men because it is harder to see them. If you are a woman, inspecting your vulva (external genital organs) by putting a mirror between your legs and looking is a good idea. That way, you can be familiar with how your vagina typically looks and feels. If you feel any itching, pain, or discomfort, you can inspect your vulva for signs of an infection. However, if you are sexually active, get regular checkups because not all infections produce symptoms or changes in the way your vulva looks.

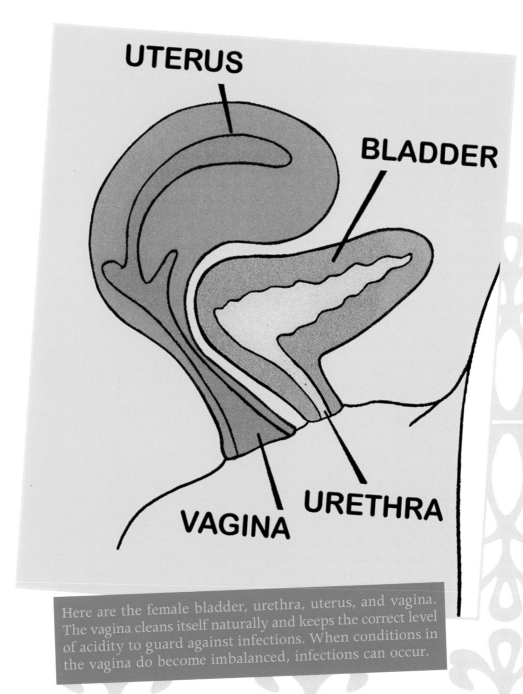

UTERUS

BLADDER

VAGINA

URETHRA

Here are the female bladder, urethra, uterus, and vagina.
The vagina cleans itself naturally and keeps the correct level
of acidity to guard against infections. When conditions in
the vagina do become imbalanced, infections can occur.

A Delicate Balance

Vaginal infections occur in women of all ages. To stay healthy, a vagina must maintain a balance between the good bacteria that are normally found there and the hormonal changes that take place in the rest of a woman's body.

The vagina is a self-cleaning organ. This means it cleans itself naturally, without assistance. Although some women choose to wash their vaginas with a douche, or jet of water containing a cleansing agent, this isn't necessary and can rid often the vagina of healthy bacteria. The walls of the vagina constantly are producing secretions of natural liquids that provide necessary moisture, keep the vagina clean, and maintain the right level of natural acidity that helps protect against infection.

Problems occur when this balance in the vaginal environment is disrupted. Such changes can be caused by many factors, including the following:

- Antibiotic or hormonal treatments
- Birth control devices
- Douches
- Some tampons
- Vaginal medications
- Sexual contact
- Sexually transmitted diseases (STDs)
- Stress
- Smoking

For women, vaginal infections are the most predominant kind of medical problem that affect their reproductive organs. When found early, they can be treated and cured without difficulty. Two vaginal infections are quite common: yeast infections and trichomoniasis. Toxic shock syndrome (TSS) can affect women, men, and children. Although quite uncommon, TSS is much more life-threatening than the other two infections.

Vaginal Yeast Infections

Vaginal yeast infections are extremely common. According to the U.S. Centers for Disease Control and Prevention (CDC), close to 80 percent of all women will experience a vaginal yeast infection at least once in their lives. Younger women, in particular, experience yeast infections. Several factors may contribute to this circumstance, including antibiotics prescribed for acne, birth control methods, pregnancy, menstruation, and tight underwear. By the time they have turned twenty-five, an estimated 50 percent of American college students have had at least one yeast infection.

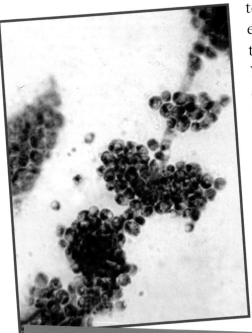

This is *Candida albicans*, which usually lives in the vagina. The fungus only causes infection if it becomes overgrown.

When you hear the word "yeast," you probably think of the slightly sweet-smelling powder that is used to make bread rise. This is the most popular variety of yeast, which is actually a fungus. Other species of yeast also live in our bodies. One of the most common is *Candida*. Around 80 percent of yeast infections, or *Candidiasis*, are caused by a certain type of *Candida* known as *Candida albicans*. Other, less common varieties of *Candida* are responsible for the remaining 20 percent of yeast infections.

When your vagina is healthy, with all its bacteria living in balance, *Candida* doesn't create trouble. Yet changes to this delicate environment—brought about by anything from stress, to injury, to sexual activity—can cause the yeast to multiply. Yeast receives nourishment from glucose, which is a form of sugar produced by your body. Any occurrence that increases your blood sugar, or changes the hormonal balance that regulates blood sugar, can make yeast grow out of control. Yeast infections can make you feel itchy and uncomfortable. The good news is that they usually are easy to treat.

Trichomoniasis

Trichomoniasis, more popularly known as "trich," is a typical vaginal infection. The National Institute of Allergy and Infectious Diseases (NIAID) estimates that five million new cases occur each year in the United States, and 170 million cases occur worldwide. Trichomoniasis is considered an STD. It is caused by a tiny, single-celled parasite called *Trichomonas vaginalis*, which travels from one person's sex organs to another during sexual intercourse or through the exchange of sexual fluids.

Although they affect both women and men, trich's symptoms are more common in women. They usually appear in the vagina, whereas in men the most common site of infection is the urethra (urine canal). When a woman's vaginal environment is out of balance, she is vulnerable to infection. While women can acquire trich from sexual contact with women and men, women usually only infect men. Trichomoniasis and its main symptoms—irritation, itching (worse for women than men), and a strong smell—are unpleasant, but easily curable.

Toxic Shock Syndrome

Unlike yeast infections and trichomoniasis, toxic shock syndrome is a very rare infection of the vagina, but it is also very serious. TSS is a systemic illness, which means that it affects the entire body's system. If unchecked, it can attack internal organs such as the kidneys and liver, causing them to go into shock and stop functioning.

Two types of bacteria cause TSS: *Staphylococcus aureus* and *Streptococcus pyogenes*. They frequently live on the skin of one in every three healthy people, and in the nose, armpits, crotch, and vagina. TSS is more often caused by *Staphylococcus aureus*. When gazed at under a microscope, these bacteria look like a tiny cluster of golden grapes. Their distinctive color accounts for the bacteria's nickname, "golden staph." (*Aureus* is the Latin word for "gold.")

Certain strains of these bacteria can produce toxins. A toxin is a protein that is poisonous. Every year in the United States, some 500,000 people contract a staphylococcal infection. If it occurs on the surface of the skin, it can be quite mild, producing nothing more than a pimple or boil. Most people's bodies have a natural defense system, or antibodies, which fights these toxins. However, a few people don't have these antibodies. If the bacteria somehow

In the 1970s, toxic shock syndrome was linked to the use of super-absorbent tampons. Once feminine hygiene products and habits improved, the number of TSS cases linked to menstruation decreased.

enter the body through a wound or orifice, enter the bloodstream, and come into contact with internal organs, they can cause life-threatening diseases such as pneumonia and TSS.

In many cases of TSS, the bacteria infect a woman's vagina. In fact, when many people think of TSS, they think of tampons. In the late 1970s, when the first cases of the illness began to be known, TSS was linked to the use of super-absorbent tampons. After research led to better tampons and improved feminine hygiene habits (such as changing tampons more frequently), the number of TSS cases decreased enormously. Currently, less than a dozen cases are reported each year to the CDC, and only around

MYTHS &

MYTH Any vaginal odor is a bad thing.

FACT Most women have a normal vaginal odor that comes and goes during the monthly menstrual cycle. It can change based on personal hygiene, hormone levels, use of birth control pills, and an imbalance of normal vaginal bacteria or yeast. Only a really strong or fishy odor is a sign of a vaginal infection.

MYTH It's possible to lose something in your vagina.

FACT Many women have difficulty removing objects, like tampons, from their vaginas. However, the vagina is a closed-ended channel and is only 3 to 5 inches deep. If you have trouble removing something, a change of position can help.

MYTH Once I've had a yeast infection, trichomoniasis, or toxic shock syndrome, I can never get it again.

FACT Wrong. Many women have yeast infections more than once. You can get infected with trichomoniasis numerous times, especially if you have a male partner who can re-infect you if he doesn't seek treatment. Women who have had toxic shock syndrome once have a 30 to 40 percent chance of getting it again.

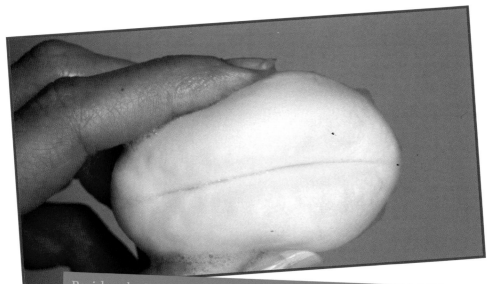

Besides the TSS cases that have been linked to tampon use, some have been connected to the use of the contraceptive sponge, such as the one shown here, and another birth control method, the diaphragm.

50 percent of all TSS cases are vaginal ones linked to menstruation. Of these cases of menstrual TSS, most are linked to tampon use, but a few have been linked to the use of two birth control methods: the diaphragm and the contraceptive sponge, both of which are inserted into the vagina. Although TSS generally is associated with women, men and children can get it as well. In the case of men and children, toxins usually enter the body via open wounds, burns, insect bites, or following surgery.

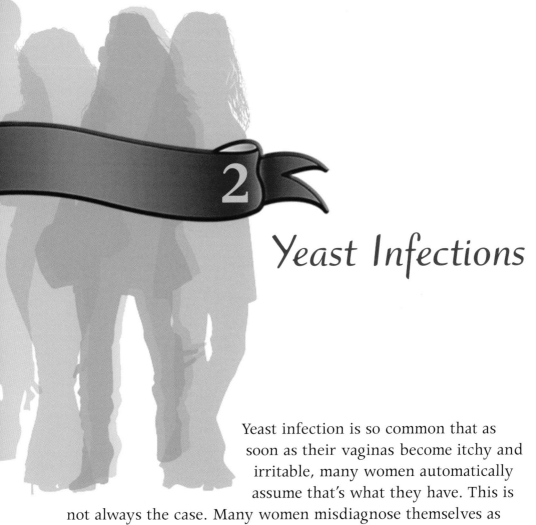

2

Yeast Infections

Yeast infection is so common that as soon as their vaginas become itchy and irritable, many women automatically assume that's what they have. This is not always the case. Many women misdiagnose themselves as having yeast infections, when they actually have another form of vaginal infection that could be more serious. In a 2002 study, published in the *Journal of Obstetrics and Gynecology*, only 33 percent of women who were treating themselves for a yeast infection actually had one. For this reason, if you suspect you have a yeast infection, or something else, make an appointment to see a doctor who can give you a professional diagnosis.

Symptoms

Yeast infections can be mild or severe. In general, symptoms include vaginal itching, soreness, and a burning sensation that

A doctor can detect a yeast infection by performing a physical examination and by taking a sample from the infected area to check under a microscope. Most yeast infections are easy to cure, as long as they are not acute infections.

you'll feel when you urinate. Sometimes the vaginal itching can be so bad that it might be extremely uncomfortable to ride a bike or walk. Your vagina and vulva will become irritated, with rashes or redness on the skin outside the vagina. Having sexual intercourse will be extremely painful. You also will be able to detect a white or white-gray discharge that smells like the yeast found in beer and freshly baked bread. Thick and lumpy, this discharge—known as garria—often resembles ricotta or cottage cheese. More infrequently, garria might be yellowish in color and be more of a clear liquid than a solid.

Diagnosis

Although the symptoms of yeast infection are usually obvious, it is always best to get a doctor's opinion, especially if it is your first occurrence. A doctor can diagnose a yeast infection by examining you and then taking a swab of the infected area. When placing the sample under a microscope, the doctor can see the presence of the *Candida* fungi. If a large number of fungi are detectable, this is proof that you have a yeast infection.

Treatment

Yeast infections are almost always simple to cure. Treatment, however, depends on how severe the infection is. Minor infections can be treated with home remedies. For more serious cases, you'll need to buy an over-the-counter (non-prescription) medication from your local drugstore, or else get a doctor's prescription for a stronger antifungal medication. Antifungal drugs that are used to fight yeast infections usually are lotions that are applied to the infected area or suppositories (cylindrical-shaped capsules containing medicine) that are inserted into the vagina. For more serious or re-occurring yeast infections, there are antifungal pills that can fight yeast.

Home Treatments

If you pay close attention to how your body looks and feels, you can detect a yeast infection in its early stages. At that time, you often can stop the fungi from expanding by using a do-it-your-self treatment.

A popular home remedy for treating yeast infections is the use of plain yogurt. Yogurt contains the bacteria called *Lactobacillus acidophilus*, which can help kill the *Candida* fungus.

One of the most popular and efficient home remedies for yeast infections is yogurt. In fact, yogurt works so well that many doctors recommend it. Yogurt contains bacteria called *Lactobacillus acidophilus* that also is found in healthy vaginas. When it comes into contact with the yeast, the *acidophilus* kills the *Candida*. You should apply the yogurt (some women dip a tampon in the yogurt) directly to your infected vaginal region once or twice per day until your symptoms clear up. Make sure that you use only plain, unflavored yogurt with no sugar that contains live *acidophilus* culture (available in health food stores and many supermarkets). Eating yogurt—a lot—is another good way to ward off and help clear up yeast infections. You can buy *acidophilus* tablets or capsules at a health food store.

Fresh garlic is another commonly used, natural antifungal substance that kills off yeast. After peeling off all the paper-thin skin from a fresh garlic clove, insert it in your vagina and leave it there for several hours or overnight. Try putting a fresh clove inside your vagina every morning and night. There is no need to worry that it will get lost because the garlic can't get through your cervix.

Over-the-Counter Treatments

Over-the-counter treatments are more powerful medications that you can buy at a drugstore without a doctor's prescription. Always see a doctor and make sure that you really do have a yeast infection before buying one of these medications. If you use one and don't have a yeast infection, you can create new drug-resistant yeast in your crotch. When you do have a yeast infection, many over-the-counter medications won't be able to kill the fungi.

The most popular over-the-counter yeast infection medications are sold as vaginal creams or suppositories (cylindrical-shaped capsules containing medicine). The creams are inserted into your vagina using an applicator similar to that of a tampon. The suppositories also are inserted into your vagina, where their casings will melt, allowing the medication inside to work against the infection. Leading over-the-counter medications include the following:

Drug	Brand Name
Miconazole	(Monistat-7, M-Zole)
Tioconazole	(Vagistat Vaginal)
Butoconazole	(Femstat)
Clotrimazole	(Femizole-7, Gyne-Lotrimin)

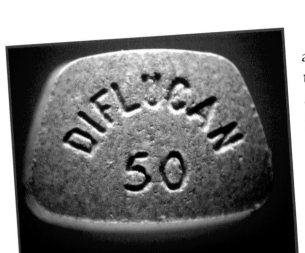

Doctors prescribe Fluconazole to treat yeast infections. The length of treatment depends on your condition and response to the drug.

These antifungal drugs are used between two and ten days and usually are applied at night before going to bed. You also can buy anti-itch creams that will relieve your discomfort. While most women experience improvement within just a few days, it's important to finish the entire treatment to make sure that all the fungi have been killed and to avoid a recurrence. If any irritation occurs, you should stop using the medication right away. These non-prescription drugs clear up yeast infections in 75 to 90 percent of cases. If symptoms continue without improvement for more than a week, see your doctor. You either have a very severe yeast infection or another type of vaginal infection.

Prescription Treatments

If your doctor confirms that you have a severe yeast infection, he or she will probably give you a written prescription for one of the following medications:

Drug	Brand Name
Itraconazole	Sporanox
Fluconazole	Diflucan

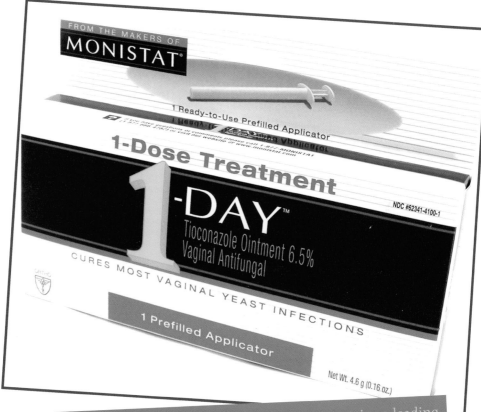

Monistat-1 cream, a one-dose treatment, contains a leading over-the-counter drug, Tioconazole, which is used in ointments to treat many vaginal yeast infections.

Terconazole   Terazole
Ketaconazole   Nizarole

These powerful medications come in pill or capsule form and are taken in one dose, or else they are creams that can be applied directly to the skin. Since they are so strong, some women may experience side effects ranging from skin irritations (in the case

10 Great Questions to Ask Your Doctor About Yeast Infections, Trichomoniasis, and Toxic Shock Syndrome

1 What are the most common signs of a yeast infection?

2 Because I am a male with a yeast infection, can I be treated with a medication that has been prescribed for a vaginal yeast infection?

3 If I have a vaginal yeast infection once, can I get one again?

4 How can I avoid getting yeast infections in the future?

5 How did I get trichomoniasis, and what are my treatment options?

6 Am I at risk for other infections if I have trichomoniasis?

7 How will I know that my trichomoniasis has been cured?

8 How serious is toxic shock syndrome, and will I have to be hospitalized?

9 Are medications prescribed for toxic shock syndrome? Are there any side effects to these medicines?

10 How can I avoid getting toxic shock syndrome?

of creams) to headaches, fever, and other flu-like symptoms (in the case of pills).

Male Yeast Infections

Men, too, can get yeast infections—on their penises. The most common way men get yeast infections is by having unprotected sex with a woman who has a yeast infection. Unlike a woman, when a man gets a yeast infection, it is rare that he will see or feel any symptoms. For this reason, an infected man can re-infect a female partner, even after she has been treated. Uncircumcised males, or males with intact foreskins on their penises, are more likely to get a yeast infection than those who are circumcised.

In the rare event that a man does experience symptoms, they are often as irritating as those that women have. Aside from the presence of white discharge, red and irritated skin, plus tiny blisters on the head of the penis, men can experience soreness, pain, and severe itching. The only treatment for male yeast infection is seeing a doctor and getting a prescription for one of the same antifungal medications used by women for yeast infections.

Risk Factors

Although you can get a vaginal yeast infection at any age, it is most common in younger women during their childbearing years. Women who are pregnant; diabetic; who are taking antibiotics, birth control pills, or steroids (which contain hormones that can upset the vaginal ecosystem); or who have a weakened immune system (which is the case of many people with the human immunodeficiency virus, or HIV) are more likely to get yeast infections, as well as repeat yeast infections that may not clear up easily with proper treatment. These factors, along with vaginal injuries, hormonal changes (especially around menstruation time), and sexual contact, all increase the risks of disrupting the vaginal environment and leading to the multiplication of yeast, which can turn into an infection.

Prevention

Some factors that are favorable to yeast infections you can't do anything about. Others you can. Wearing clothes, especially underpants or bikinis, which are tight, dirty, sweaty, or made from non-cotton materials that trap heat and moisture can contribute to your getting a yeast infection. Avoid tight underwear and pantyhose. Because yeast can live in your underwear, you should wash your panties well and change them regularly.

Chemicals such as inks, dyes, and perfumes can upset your vaginal environment or create allergies that lead to yeast infections. Scented douches and other vaginal soaps and scents that you can buy at the drugstore can lead to yeast infections. Perfumed and/or dyed toilet paper, scented tampons or sanitary pads, female deodorant sprays, and even some laundry detergents can cause them, too. In general, the more chemicals and artificial products you keep away from your vagina, the better off you'll be. Condoms coated with a lubricant containing the sperm-killing drug Nonoxynol-9 and flavored condoms also have been linked to yeast infections.

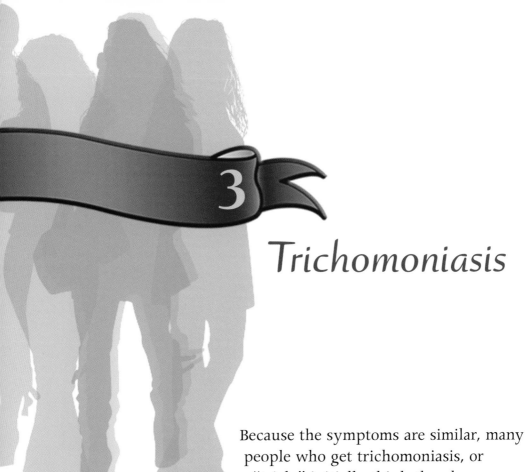

3

Trichomoniasis

Because the symptoms are similar, many people who get trichomoniasis, or "trich," initially think they have a yeast infection. Although not as common as yeast infections, trichomoniasis affects around five million Americans each year, around half of them women. It generally is considered to be an STD because it is frequently passed from one person to another during sexual intercourse. However, it is not impossible to come into contact with the trich parasites that thrive in warm and wet environments, in places such as public baths, hot tubs, or moist towels.

Symptoms

Trichomoniasis often occurs without symptoms. Men rarely have symptoms, and around 20 percent of women show no symptoms,

These young people are enjoying a relaxing moment in a whirlpool tub. Trichomoniasis parasites can flourish in warm, wet hot tubs, and can be spread through the contact of moist towels or wet clothing.

either. When women do have symptoms, they usually get them between one and four weeks after being infected. The symptoms in women include a heavy, yellow-green or gray vaginal discharge with a strong odor, as well as pain during sexual intercourse and urination. Irritation and itching of the vagina and surrounding area, and pain in the lower abdomen, can occur also. When men experience symptoms, the most common ones are a watery, white discharge from the penis, and pain during urination or ejaculation.

Laboratory tests using a microscope are performed on samples so that researchers can discern whether the *Trichomonas vaginalis* parasite is present in specimens.

Diagnosis

To get a positive diagnosis of trichomoniasis, you need to see a health-care provider. He or she will examine you, looking for signs of infection. Aside from the symptoms mentioned previously, women often have small, red sores on the insides of their vagina. The doctor will take a sample of the discharge from the vagina or penis for a laboratory test. A microscope will reveal the presence of the tiny *Trichomonas vaginalis* parasite, which is usually harder to detect in men than in women.

Treatment

Most cases of trichomoniasis can be cured using the prescription drug metronidazole. This medication comes in pill or capsule form. A strong, single dose is usually all that is required to kill the trich parasite. In many men, symptoms may disappear without treatment in a few weeks. If he has never had any symptoms, an infected man still can infect or re-infect a female partner. So, for safety's sake, he should be treated, too. Having trich once doesn't mean you can't get it again. Therefore, you and any partner shouldn't have sex until your treatment is complete and all symptoms have disappeared. Untreated, trichomoniasis can be harmful to pregnant women by causing preterm delivery or rupturing the membranes that protect the unborn baby. Women who are not pregnant are more likely to contract HIV without treatment.

Risk Factors and Prevention

The only sure-fire method of not getting an STD, including trichomoniasis, is not to have sex. The next best thing is to use a latex condom every time you have sex.

If you discover you have trichomoniasis, inform all of the sexual partners you have had within the past three months so they can be tested and treated as well. To be on the safe side, if you get treated, your partner should, too. Having an STD is

Using latex condoms can help protect you against sexually transmitted diseases, including trichomoniasis.

nothing to be ashamed of. If you have one, get it treated. Being mature enough to have sex means being mature enough to deal with its sometimes-unpleasant consequences. Even if you only had sex with someone once, suggesting that he or she get tested is the healthy thing to do. Wouldn't you want a partner to be in touch with you if he or she discovered an STD?

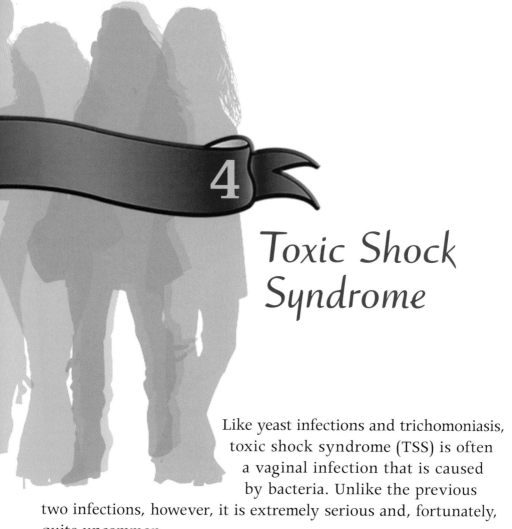

Toxic Shock Syndrome

Like yeast infections and trichomoniasis, toxic shock syndrome (TSS) is often a vaginal infection that is caused by bacteria. Unlike the previous two infections, however, it is extremely serious and, fortunately, quite uncommon.

There are two bacteria that cause TSS: *Staphylococcus aureus* and *Streptococcus pyogenes*. The much rarer form of TSS caused by *Streptococcus* bacteria is streptococcal toxic shock syndrome (STSS).

Symptoms

The main symptoms of TSS will appear between twenty-four and forty-eight hours following infection by *Staphylococcus* or *Streptococcus* bacteria. Because the infection is caused by a toxin, or poison produced by the bacteria, many of the body's internal

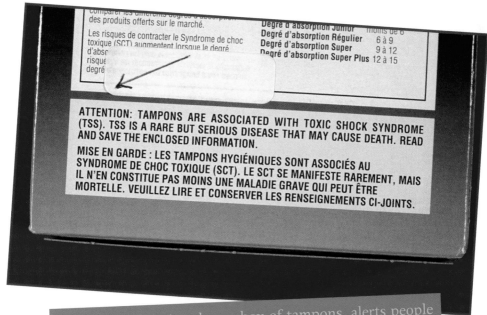

comparer les différents degrés d'absorption
des produits offerts sur le marché.

Les risques de contracter le Syndrome de choc
toxique (SCT) augmentent lorsque le degré
d'absc
risque
degré

Degré d'absorption Junior   moins de 6
Degré d'absorption Régulier   6 à 9
Degré d'absorption Super   9 à 12
Degré d'absorption Super Plus 12 à 15

ATTENTION: TAMPONS ARE ASSOCIATED WITH TOXIC SHOCK SYNDROME (TSS). TSS IS A RARE BUT SERIOUS DISEASE THAT MAY CAUSE DEATH. READ AND SAVE THE ENCLOSED INFORMATION.

MISE EN GARDE : LES TAMPONS HYGIÉNIQUES SONT ASSOCIÉS AU SYNDROME DE CHOC TOXIQUE (SCT). LE SCT SE MANIFESTE RAREMENT, MAIS IL N'EN CONSTITUE PAS MOINS UNE MALADIE GRAVE QUI PEUT ÊTRE MORTELLE. VEUILLEZ LIRE ET CONSERVER LES RENSEIGNEMENTS CI-JOINTS.

This warning, printed on a box of tampons, alerts people to the risks associated with tampon use and toxic shock syndrome. *Staphylococcus* and *Streptococcus* bacteria produce a toxin that can damage internal organs.

organs will be affected as the bacteria move through the bloodstream. As these essential organs begin to suffer damage, the following will occur:

- Headaches and muscle aches
- Sore throat
- Feeling of faintness or lightheadedness (caused by a rapid drop in blood pressure)
- Diarrhea
- Vomiting
- Sudden, high fever (with a temperature of 102 degrees Fahrenheit or more)

- Rash that resembles sunburn
- Bloodshot eyes and a strange redness under the eyelids or inside the mouth or vagina
- Broken blood vessels that may appear on your skin
- Unusual vaginal discharge or strange vaginal odor

Symptoms of toxic shock syndrome can include a headache, muscle aches, and feelings of faintness or lightheadedness.

Other symptoms may include: confusion; tiredness and weakness; a fast, but weakened, pulse; thirst; rapid breathing; and skin that looks pale and feels cool and clammy.

In the extremely rare cases of TSS caused by the *Streptococcus* bacteria (STSS), within forty-eight hours your blood pressure will drop dangerously, leaving you feeling dizzy, confused, and feverish, with breathing problems and a weak, but rapid, pulse. Aside from cool, moist skin, you may have a blotchy rash that peels. Because with STSS most bacteria infect the body via a skin injury or open wound (such as a cut, scrape, or chickenpox blisters), the area around the infection or wound will become red and swollen. Quickly, the skin surrounding the wound will become severely damaged.

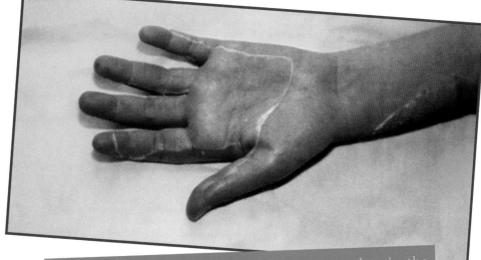

A sign of toxic shock syndrome that occurs late in the development of the disease is the peeling of the skin, which is evident on this individual's palm.

Signs of Shock

With both types of toxic shock syndrome, as the toxins released by the bacteria enter the bloodstream, bleeding problems may occur and liver and kidneys might start to fail, causing your body to go into shock.

Of the symptoms mentioned above, certain ones are signs that your body is beginning to go into shock. Since this could be fatal, get to a hospital as fast as you can if you notice any of the following:

- Cold hands and feet
- Fast, but weak, pulse

- Confusion or other mental disturbances
- Pale, moist skin
- Shortness of breath or abnormally rapid breathing
- Overwhelming feeling of anxiety or fear

Diagnosis

Because symptoms of TSS are sudden and serious, see a doctor immediately, especially if you detect signs of shock. Doctors diagnose both TSS and STSS by doing a physical exam and carrying out blood tests that can check how well your liver and kidneys are functioning. They also will take samples of fluid from infected wounds and place them under a microscope to detect the presence of *Staphylococcus* or *Streptococcus* bacteria.

Treatment

Treatment for TSS must begin immediately at the intensive care unit of a hospital. The most common treatment is antibiotic medication that will kill the bacteria. In very serious cases, a doctor might prescribe steroids. However, your doctor may need to drain any infected wounds beforehand.

While under treatment, you will stay at the hospital for several days. You'll be closely monitored by your doctor for signs of shock, blood pressure or breathing problems, or organ damage. You should be released only when all symptoms have disappeared. To keep blood pressure at a normal rate and to clear up other symptoms, you may need to take other medications and receive fluids intravenously, through a needle. In cases of STSS where

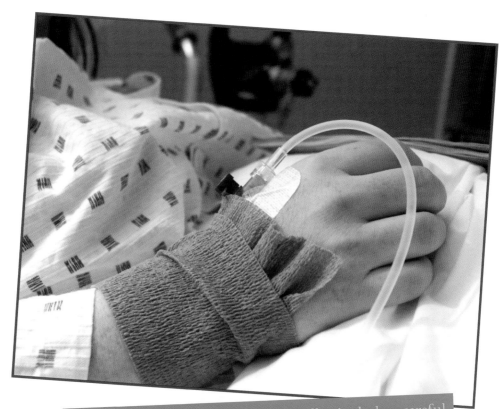

Hospital treatment for TSS typically includes careful monitoring and antibiotic medication that will be used to destroy the bacteria. In serious cases of TSS, steroids are prescribed to patients.

there has been a lot of skin damage, surgery may be necessary to remove the dead skin and muscles surrounding an infected wound. With proper treatment, patients usually recover from TSS and STSS in two to three weeks.

Risk Factors and Prevention

If you're a girl who has just started getting her period, you may have heard scary stories about TSS and its links to tampons. The truth is that the tampons made today are much safer than the high-absorbency ones made with polyester beads twenty to thirty years ago. However, if you choose to use tampons when you first start menstruating, buy those that have the lowest absorbency and change them frequently. If you've ever had TSS or a *Staphylococcus* infection, don't use tampons or birth control devices linked to it, like diaphragms and contraceptive sponges.

Wash your hands before and after inserting a tampon. At night, insert a fresh tampon before you go to bed and remove it when you wake up in the morning. Ideally, you should change tampons every four to eight hours. If you use tampons and notice an unusual vaginal discharge or any strange odors, see a doctor immediately.

Although around 50 percent of TSS cases are linked to menstruation and tampon use, men and children, as well as women, can get it through open wounds, burns, insect bites, or following surgery. Both sexes and all ages can acquire TSS, but women who have already had the disease are at the greatest risk, as the recurrence rate is reported to increase between 30 and 40 percent. Surprisingly, TSS in men and women often occurs in healthy, younger people between the ages of twenty and fifty.

Cases of STSS can occur via open wounds and infections, including those acquired during surgery. For this reason, always clean and bandage all skin wounds, including scrapes and cuts, as soon as possible. If a wound becomes red, swollen, tender, and causes a fever, see a doctor right away.

5

Making Progress

Progress is being made in terms of the medical community's knowledge of yeast infections, trichomoniasis, and toxic shock syndrome. As more people become informed, it is simpler to prevent these infections and diagnose and treat them in their milder, early stages. At the same time, treatments have become easier and more efficient.

Yeast Infections

It is inevitable that most women will have a yeast infection at least once in their lives. However, increased knowledge about the infections allows more to avoid them or check them before they get serious. For example, many women know not to use vaginal douches, scented sanitary products and feminine deodorants, and to stay clear of tight underwear made of non-cotton fabrics containing dyes, all of which can provoke yeast infections.

Medical researchers, such as these at the Centers for Disease Control and Prevention, are constantly looking for effective and efficient ways to identify various bacteria and viruses to improve treatment options.

Before 1990, women could only treat vaginal yeast infections by going to a doctor and getting a prescription for medication. Today, there are an increasing number of over-the-counter treatments that you can buy at your drugstore. The drugs most commonly used to treat yeast infections are "azoles." They break down the cell walls of the *Candida* organisms, causing the fungi to dissolve completely. Although these drugs are efficient, severe yeast infections require stronger antifungal medication. Furthermore, some infections become resistant to antifungal drugs, particularly when women use them repeatedly or for conditions that turn out not to be yeast infections. A current medical challenge is to discover new medication that can treat these more resistant infections.

The benefit of the greater number of over-the-counter medications means that women no longer have to suffer while waiting to get a doctor's appointment. However, women who choose to diagnose and treat themselves should be careful. Studies estimate that up to 60 percent of women who have purchased over-the-counter antifungal medication did not, in fact, have a yeast infection. Because a mistaken diagnosis can lead to other drug-resistant infections, women suffering from yeast infection symptoms for the first time should receive a diagnosis from a doctor before taking any medication.

Trichomoniasis

With increased sex education and preventive measures taken to avoid trichomoniasis and other STDs, there has been a significant decrease over the last thirty years in the number of cases in North America. According to CDC data, doctors diagnosed 427,000 cases of vaginal trichomoniasis in 1974. In 2004, that number was 221,000.

Until recently, men and women who suffered from trichomoniasis in the United States only had the option of one kind of treatment: the drug metronidazole. However, in May 2004, the U.S. Food and Drug Administration (FDA), the government agency responsible for monitoring drugs and medication for use by the public, approved a new drug for the treatment of trichomoniasis. Tinidazole, sold under the brand name Tindamax, was the first new treatment in forty years. It has worked for those few patients who don't respond well to metronidazole and for people who have recurrent or more resistant forms of trichomoniasis. Taken in a single pill along with food, it has proven to be

Proper sex education and learning about the various measures to prevent yeast infections, trichomoniasis, and toxic shock syndrome will help today's young people to avoid such illnesses.

highly efficient, curing 96 percent of cases in women and 94 percent in men.

Toxic Shock Syndrome

In the last twenty years, cases of TSS have diminished significantly in North America. Improvements in tampons, better education about hygiene, changing tampons more frequently, washing hands before and after changing tampons, and keeping wounds clean have made an impact by creating fewer situations through which either *Staphylococcus* or *Streptococcus* bacteria can infect the bloodstream.

In fact, TSS is so rare that most doctors will never come across a case during their entire medical careers. The highest number of TSS cases in the United States occurred between 1979 and 1980, during which there were about six to twelve cases per 100,000 people. Many were due to the use of a brand of super-absorbent tampon, which is no longer produced. Since then, there has been a marked decrease in the number of cases. According to CDC data, the number of cases of menstrual-related TSS has dropped enormously: from 814 in 1980 to 5 in 1997. Only 5 percent of cases are fatal.

One of the big challenges facing scientists is discovering an antibody, a protein created by the body that acts as a natural defense against foreign bacteria, which could defeat the toxins released by the *Staphylococcus* and *Streptococcus* bacteria. Studies have shown that many TSS patients, particularly women, find themselves with fewer or no antibodies following their illness. This absence of TSS antibodies in women puts them at greater risk of developing TSS again.

Ultimately, as science advances and we grow increasingly aware of our bodies, our environment, and how they affect each other, infections caused by fungi, parasites, and bacteria should diminish. Although medicine can play an important role in treating conditions such as yeast infections, trichomoniasis, TSS, when it comes to prevention, it's up to each of us to make a difference.

Glossary

antibiotic Chemical substances, such as penicillin, produced by microorganisms and fungi that, when diluted, destroy bacteria and other disease-causing microorganisms.

antibodies Proteins created by the body that act as a natural defense against the foreign bacteria that create infections and diseases.

bacteria Single-cell, spherical, oval, or rod-shaped microorganisms that live in plants and animals, including humans.

cervix Narrow outer end of the uterus.

contraceptive sponge Small, absorbent pad that contains a spermicide and is positioned against the cervix of the uterus before sexual intercourse to prevent pregnancy.

diaphragm Thin, dome-shaped device, usually made of rubber, which is placed over the cervix to prevent pregnancy during sexual intercourse.

discharge To pour out or flow out; an emission.

douche Jet of water, often containing medicinal or cleansing agents, that is used to wash a body part, usually the vagina.

fungus Parasitic, plantlike organisms such as mushrooms, molds, mildew, and yeast that live by decomposing and absorbing the organic material in which they grow.

misdiagnosis Incorrect or mistaken conclusion regarding an illness.

over-the-counter Any commercially sold brand medication purchased without a doctor's prescription.

parasite Organism that lives on or in another species, known as the host, and survives by taking nourishment from the host's body.

prescription Direction by a doctor to a pharmacist for the preparation and use of a medication.

steroids Hormones produced by the body's adrenal glands and reproductive organs; also chemically manufactured compounds (known as corticosteroids) used as medication for people whose bodies can't produce steroids naturally.

suppository Conically or cylindrically shaped capsule full of medication that melts after being inserted into the vagina or rectum.

swab Small piece of material used to clean wounds, apply medications, or retrieve samples of body fluids.

tampon Plug of absorbent material inserted into a body cavity or wound to check blood flow or absorb secretions; especially used in the vagina during menstruation.

yeast Small, single-celled fungi that are capable of fermenting carbohydrates into alcohol and carbon dioxide (used for making bread and beer).

For More Information

ASHA's STI Resource Center
(800) 227-8922

> This hotline plays recordings about STI information twenty-four hours a day and has specialists who answer questions from 9 AM to 6 PM, EST, Monday through Friday.

Centers for Disease Control and Prevention (CDC)
1600 Clifton Road
Atlanta, GA 30333
(404) 639-3534 / (800) 311-3435
Web site: http://www.cdc.gov/az.do

> This U.S. government organization provides up-to-date information, research, statistics, and advice about all types of diseases and infections, as well as treatment options.

Go Ask Alice
Web site: http://www.goaskalice.columbia.edu

> A site for young people run by the Health Education program at Columbia University. It has a Q&A section and a database on numerous health topics, including sexual health.

I Wanna Know
Web site: http://www.iwannaknow.org

> This teen Web site produced by the American Social Health Association (ASHA) offers FAQs, advice, links, and discussion groups for teens concerning all sorts of health issues.

National Institute of Allergy and Infectious Diseases (NIAID)
6610 Rockledge Drive, MSC 6612
Bethesda, MD 20892-6612
(301) 496-5717
Web site: http://www.niaid.nih.gov/default.htm

NIAID promotes research to better understand, treat, and prevent infectious and allergic diseases. Its work has led to new therapies, vaccines, diagnostic tests, and other technologies that have improved the health of millions around the world.

Teens' Health
Web site: http://www.kidshealth.org/teen

Sponsored by the Nemours Foundation, this site provides teens with information and advice by medical experts pertaining to psychological and physical health issues.

The Yeast Infection Home Page
Web site: http://www.msu.edu/~eisthen/yeast

An often humorous, fact-filled, and very thorough source that deals with every aspect of yeast infection, it offers lots of useful links.

Web Sites

Due to the changing nature of Internet links, Rosen Publishing has developed an online list of Web sites related to the subject of this book. This site is updated regularly. Please use this link to access the list:

http://www.rosenlinks.com/gh/yits

For Further Reading

Bell, Ruth. *Changing Bodies, Changing Lives* (3rd Ed.). New York, NY: Three Rivers Press, 1998.

Boston Women's Health Book Collective. *Our Bodies, Ourselves: A New Edition for a New Era*. New York, NY: Simon & Schuster, 2005.

Favor, Lesli J. *Bacteria*. (The Library of Disease-Causing Organisms). New York, NY: Rosen, 2004.

Gravelle, Karen. *The Period Book* (Updated Ed.). New York, NY: Walker Books, 2006.

Gravelle, Karen. *What's Going on Down There? Answers to Questions Boys Find Hard to Ask*. New York, NY: Walker Books, 1998.

Harris, Robie. *It's Perfectly Normal: Changing Bodies, Growing Up, Sex, and Sexual Health* (10th Anniversary Ed.). Cambridge, MA: Candlewick Press, 2004.

Wider, Jennifer. *The Doctor's Complete College Girls' Health Guide: From Sex to Drugs to the Freshman Fifteen*. New York, NY: Bantam Books, 2006.

Bibliography

Centers for Disease Control and Prevention (CDC). "Toxic Shock Syndrome." "Trichomoniasis." Retrieved February 2007 (http://www.cdc.gov).

DermNet NZ. "Toxic Shock Syndrome." Retrieved February 2007 (http://www.dermnet.org.nz/bacterial/toxic-shock-syndrome.html).

Good, Jonni. "What Is a Yeast Infection?" EzineArticles. January 29, 2007. Retrieved February 2007 (http://ezinearticles.com/?What-Is-A-Yeast-Infection?&id=435535).

KidsHealth. "Toxic Shock Syndrome." "Trichomoniasis." "Vaginal Yeast Infections." Retrieved February 2007 (http://www.kidshealth.org).

Lite, J. "Vaginal Infections: Female Trouble." Retrieved February 2007 (http://www.health-help4dumbbells.com/Vaginal_Infections.html).

Toxic Shock Syndrome Information Service. Retrieved February 2007 (http://www.toxicshock.com/).

The Yeast Infection Home Page. Modified February 29, 2004. Retrieved August 2006. (http://www.msu.edu/~eisthen/yeast).

Index

A

antibiotics, 8, 9, 23

C

Candida, 10, 17, 18, 38

H

human immunodeficiency virus
(HIV), 24, 28

J

*Journal of Obstetrics and
Gynecology*, 15

N

National Institute of Allergy and
Infectious Diseases (NIAID), 10

S

Staphylococcus aureus, 11, 30, 34,
36, 40
Streptococcus pyogenes, 11, 30, 32,
34–36, 40

T

toxic shock syndrome (TSS)
causes of, 11–12, 14

and contraceptives, 14, 36
diagnosis, 33–34
and men/children, 9, 14, 36
risk factors/preventing, 36, 40
symptoms, 30–34
and tampons, 12, 14, 36, 40–41
treating, 12, 22, 34–35, 40
Trichomonas vaginalis, 10, 28
trichomoniasis
causes of, 10, 25
commonality of, 4, 9, 10, 25
diagnosing, 27–28
and men, 4, 10–11, 25–26
misdiagnosing, 25
risk factors/preventing, 28–29
symptoms, 10–11, 25–27
treating, 11, 22, 28, 39–40

Y

yeast infections
causes of, 9–10
commonality of, 4, 9, 15
diagnosing, 15, 17, 39
and men, 4–6, 22, 23
misdiagnosing, 5, 15, 39
risk factors/preventing, 18,
22–24, 37
symptoms, 10, 15–16, 22, 23
treating, 17–21, 23, 38–39